T0099517

The Palace of Bones

The Palace of Bones

Allison Eir Jenks

OHIO UNIVERSITY PRESS

ATHENS

Ohio University Press, Athens, Ohio 45701
© 2002 by Allison Eir Jenks
Printed in the United States of America
All rights reserved

Ohio University Press books are printed on acid-free paper ⊗™

10 09 08 07 06 05 04 03 02   5 4 3 2 1

Library of Congress Cataloging-in-Publication Data
Jenks, Allison Eir.
     The palace of bones : poems / by Allison Eir Jenks.
          p. cm.
     ISBN 0-8214-1423-2 (acid-free paper) — ISBN 0-8214-1424-0
(pbk. : acid-free paper)
     I. Title.

PS3560.E5147 P35 2001
811'.54—dc21

                                        2001036427

Acknowledgments

I would like to thank the editors of the journals and anthologies in which various poems first appeared: *Salmagundi, Willow Springs, Columbia* (New York), *Michigan Quarterly Review, Massachusetts Review, Kalliope, Poetry Ireland Review, Puerto del Sol, New Orleans Review, Poet Lore, Pleiades, American Literary Review, Many Mountains Moving, Third Coast, Cyphers* (U.K.), *Stand* (U.K.), *Poets for the Millennium* (Bradshaw Books, Ireland, 1999), *Tabla Book of New Verse* (University of Bristol, England), *Introduction Series 5* (Windows Publications, Ireland, 1998), and *The Best of Pif Magazine* (Fusion Press, Texas, 1999).

The poem "Canvas" won first place in the Long Poem Section of the Scottish International Poetry Competition.

I would like to thank Paul Perry, Fred D'Aguiar, and John Balaban for their encouragement and thoughtful criticism, as well as the Tyrone Guthrie Centre in Annaghmakerrig, County Monaghan, Ireland, where many of these poems were written. I am also grateful for the James A. Michener Fellowship, which provided me the ability to start this collection.

Contents

The Palace of Bones

Forgive Us

I.

Leaving behind the voices in that city,
And whatever Mother would have said,
Or Father would have wanted.
Leaving the statues that stifle
The memory with crisp, black jaws,
The bones of their fists stiff as a rake.
How they reach to drag you from your soul,
Like slaves into their mouths, and once they have
Stolen your eyes, those good dreams
That should always have a place inside you,
They will be sure not to keep you,
And send you on your way at dawn, crippled,
But alive, with straw joints and fingers.

II.

Leaving the crickets whistling like trains,
Dragging their broken legs from under the earth.
And what people had thought of you,
To forget what they think, you must forget
Even more. The midnight hands will come
To brush the street's old breath, the half-
Written letters crumpled like white stars,
Chips of stone from the deserted church,
And if we are there we will watch the hands,

Wishing they were large enough to carry
Dead dogs from the park, the lost, the hurt,
Carry them to the sea where bones still dance.

III.

Now that I have left, Mother does nothing
But sing the words to every song I ever loved,
And Father is young and proud and whole.
The statues lower their tongues to drink
The rain and whisper my name again
And again through the tunnels and the streets
Reminding me of every dream, of every love.

The empty churches are haunted
With invisible fruit and Gods and prayers.
And the prayers shine like seeds, trespassing
Into valleys, into marble, into languages,
Into the green, the uncertainty of our hands.
The dead carry the living; the living carry the dead.
And anyone hurt will not be forgotten.

Black Magic

Already I am standing at my son's grave.
Feet numb against the stone,

The priests whispering for a song to soothe me.
The sky, half there, floods with darkness,

Folds up, wrinkled and deranged,
Humble and tired of its own mysteries.

The fever won't go down.
The moon won't go down.

My body's still full with him
And all the things that will outlast us;

Vultures, rain, pianos, even the apple trees
Reviving after the resting of the ice,

Anchored to the earth always,
Hovered above the varnished barnyards,

Stiff and strong as sleepless soldiers.
His fingers still bleed inside me.

His cradle still bleeds with life.
The night carries all the shades of the dead.

Black as black magic.

The handwriting on the grave,
The dates, sure as thunder

And wrong as God himself,
Who somehow finds time

To trim his beard and turn
His body into wine and bread.

Urns full of holy water.
The bridge is no longer there.

The magnolia is a masterpiece for death;
The iris a symbol of the ill spirit,

And I fill my mouth with them, already,
I kiss each eyelid and collect twigs

For an afternoon fire that burns,
Past the night, deserted, vexed,

Sturdy as an iron gate
Around the neck of heaven.

Waiting

After Kathy Prendergast's "Waiting"

Who with a human soul wouldn't notice
Three women against a wall with melted heads,
Dressed obediently in mother's copper gowns?
And as you were waiting for another man,
The white veils faded into liquid rust.

Of the three of you, only two breasts
Have been saved. A man is trying
To cut you out of paper into one
Woman with six perfect hands,
Hands he will keep for himself.

The rust creeps between your legs
Like large yellow fingers, to pull the wings
From each one of you. But you do not wait
As martyrs or as ghosts, you were willing
To be chosen and suffer no less now than before.

Let him think you've gone mad
As the wings beat in your hands.
Only you can remove the dresses
From the canvas in the naked dark
With your heads above the sea.

5

The Palace of Bones

Last year I hurried through
The hallways of the Louvre,
The ghosts of history confined
In one heavy album full of eyes.
The *Mona Lisa*, monarch, token
Of womanhood, the poor woman,
Strangers crowded around her
Like the hanging of a witch
And the precious Young Martyr, hands
Tied over her chest with white ribbons,
Sinking peacefully into the sea,
Bathing in death, deranged as a headless bird.
How much I was like her,
Or worse, browsing blissfully
Into her glass for my own reflection.

Even now those women trouble me,
Dancing like a string of pearls
That will never clasp; their faces,
Their footsteps never stop moving.
The Martyr dances on the evening flowers,
Drenched in the sweet smell of God
With arms white and smooth as paper.
Her rivers hang like draperies
From God's window, giving time away
So freely birds take it, drop it
And chew out its lungs. She dances

6

Into blindness like a light when you smell her.
When you reach for her hand
It tears like paper. On the paper
There is nothing but white and cold and night.

The Prisoner

What do I make of you kneeling there
Without a name and without a whole breast?
Unwilling to feed and forever in prayer,
As if you'd known the painted women in the window
All along, and how to open them without a sound.

The more we bury ourselves, the more the earth
Seems to grow back willing to let us out.
These doors weren't meant to open,
Unless you believe the mountains are overgrown animals
Or sketches of black and white.

If a woman is as close to her dream
As to her death, having to hide her body
To protect it, then she is always part prisoner.
In her trial, she has no time, no judge, no self.
She is the gavel or the frozen branch outside the window.

And not even a bird will touch her as she grows old.
Anything that outlives her will only last an hour.

8

The Visited House in Monaghan

> "I shall not drift through the streets, through the patrols like the wind of nocturnal Gdansk. Like a wounded dog my heart aches in silence—If only I knew the right word!"
>
> —*Irina Ratushinskaya*

Against this brutal light, every old prison looks like a church.
Does the wind purposely break the windows of abandoned
    houses?
I wait for the bells to signal the hour, the day.
My father could have died this morning.
No one would have told me.
There are no named roads, no accidents, no definite law.

The bells open in my sleep like someone else's past,
And this wooden house aches for life again like a madman.
But I brought my life here too late, as if a spirit
Looking back at the broken stone wall
When a war was just beginning.

I am the remnants of wars I never fought,
And don't have to know the date or the right words
To keep alive. I might have been more afraid,
And less worthy of walking these paths.
I was saved, and can hardly believe this freedom.

Boy of Sea

The boy lost himself in the woods for days
Until he was found drifting peacefully,
Fearlessly as a blanket of firelight
Atop the swamp water, alive.
Hungry, but alive and unharmed.
This God of sea, a child
We claimed had a lesser sense,
Who went about life at a slower pace,
Managed to turn his body-water into sea,
And cross hordes of snakes, wasps,
Alligators, sharks, and other sea urchins
Without provoking or frightening them.
The sea-life treaded through their routines,
And the boy drifted alongside them gracefully.

Something in the human body, perhaps,
Or the way we disguise ourselves
From the animals and from our own gods,
But still hunt against the hunters
And prowl among the prowlers,
Keeps us earthbound, apprehensive, dishonest,
Maintaining the dying things, the hunger, and the land,
With no Gods in the sea
And no angels or miracles in our way.
Drawn from the embryo toward everything perishable,
We want to believe in our own magic,
And when one of us understands the instincts

Of the larger beasts and answers to the invisible
We still let the dogs smell our fear,
And can barely hear them coming.

In Search of a Brother

As if he'd forgotten to live part of his life,
He turned the rowboat back and paddled faster.
Somewhere between earth and the ice,
He let himself breathe the incurable blue.

For a moment, time became an object,
Something that could burn the tongue
And grow inside the stomach.

The angels must all be in one place,
Brother, the birds seem to smell them
And I think I can too.

They are pure
As the scent of Mother's apron,
Smothered in syrup and lilac.

The sea stained his fingers
Like a stream of blue ink,

And every sign said something
In Italian about danger,

Though he might as well be allergic
To paper and to the sky
That hung so low he always felt
Stuck in a sick lady's living room.

Brother, all I can feel of you,
The weight of a burning house.

Slivers and demons.

The wings of the crow on fire.

Dead men in the snow.

Our childhood books,
Hot food for the earth.

The sick breath of the owls.

Can you tell me who I was twelve years ago?

Did I know God was insane?

Each of the eight lakes
Has its own ghost and God
Mating in the dry fog.

Homesick men sail by
With young boys' eyes,
Slender and delirious.

They must worship something
To keep their health, so they huddle
In a dark circle like prophets
With tea that tells the future:

Someone must die before anyone is free.

Then they toast bad liquor
And shake the tambourine.

*(I remember our lives
As if they existed in one season.)*

*A man without limbs, or was it a girl
Lying in chunks of grass as we all ran
To the church, the remnants of prayers
Hanging from our mouths like spoiled eggs.*

*Bells ringing and ringing in the dark
Like Father's voice when he was angry.*

The preacher's beard felt safe as a nest.

*Then you and Father left on a train.
Trains that lugged coal up the fields
And I could hear you squealing
Like a forbidden record*

*While Mother and I sat there
On the bench with women
Holding little cakes like children.*

As the lanterns light up on the dock
Like the eyes of a fish, he is surely in Italy.
There are more stars than an eye can carry.

Night Train from Barcelona

Now, when the basic comforts spoil—the stiff knee,
The glass of melted ice, the torn shoe—they represent failure
More than accident. They tear right into remembering.

Outside the glass doors, the distractions—
Where you started, left off, never officially ended.
I settle for brief companions, the smell of each

Tired stranger closing from his life.
One dozes off into religion, his own round spotlight,
Shining down on the Koran like a perfectly lit spirit.

Others tactfully fill the space around them with fear,
Wrapped-up belongings and invisible houses, half-lives.

On the radio, the first landing on the moon is replayed,
The conversations between Apollo and ground control;
Only eighteen seconds of fuel left, but a safe, eternal landing.

In front of me, a man who seems to follow me everywhere
Talks of fixing clocks, *Relaxing, but little profit*, he says,
As if he knew how to cheat us out of time.

Time is in synch with the speed of the train—
The sound, the climbing, the drop, the fight.
Each town we pass is too gray, too stone to be real.

During the night-haze, the night-thoughts
Where glamour appears out of darkness
Like a permanent light, a woman, too old to have a child,
Prances down the aisle with a neck-length of pearl,
Again and again until she is noticed.

A man, not from anywhere, grinds his teeth,
As if he'd bitten through the earth,
To tell us he is violent (was an unloved boy),
Knows more, will hurt you if you question him.

During each pause, each delay, like thieves we sway furiously
As if being kept from a chance, from something perfect
We have earned with the half-torn tickets in our hands.

Those who gave up believing long ago, and the ones
Still rehearsing, still waiting even to believe
In an end to this strange loneliness,
Speed toward anecdotes, a glimpse of their own histories.

By the last hour, we are all sick with entire lives
In our stomachs that we must carry now to another place,
Willing to be lost, to be strange and estranged,
To allow ourselves to live unfinished. At the end of the line,
It can be read in many ways depending on who you are,
The sign in the empty car that reads, "Nothing left to steal."

16

Canvas

I.

Magic comes and goes in handfuls
And for weeks we don't grow,
Or don't think we are growing.
We will refuse water and light,
Or swallow so much we can't speak.
Then chaos, the water is on fire.

Don't let me touch your fingers.
Don't come close enough
I can smell the death on you.
The smell is too tempting
If you know too much about it.

The old man claims he fixes clocks.
Why not leave them broken?
A clock is only an instrument.

II.

If I knew how to speak to you—
If I could write letters to you all day
And be answered in so many words—
Would life be better without reasons for it?

Let tonight answer me with angels.
Let them be stuck here, hanging
From the branches of the trees,
Then let them be movable as paper.

If I were a man, would I be less afraid?
Would stealing feel more possible?

III.

I am now in prison, raging,
With millions of bleeding wings.

At this hour, it is too late to be an arsonist.
It is too late to admit the lost;
Miles of aching road, weeds, heavy rock—
War. Black against my heart.

The heroes sit in broken chairs.
From here to the next town,
You can smell love
Like a pot of hot sauce.

Footprints flee into their doorways—
Into their long, weak halls.

IV.

I want to tell you to keep moving forward.
Full of restlessness and jealousy.

If you are dying, hold your hands still,
Behind your back. The cradle will burn.

All I can think of is the Baltic Sea,
Where all of time flows into water.

After the snow falls
And the canvas is once again white,

You'll find that everything is buried inside you.
The man you've become will never have a grave.

V.

Do you see the patches of silver grass,
Where the grapevines grow
Like broken strings from harps and violins?

Why are they tempting?
That's where it's true, those bones throbbing,
Like splinters of light. It's not the bones
That rattle, but the voices—Imagine,
Voices hungry for nothing, dried-up
Sunflowers hanging from their mouths
Only for decoration.

The bones are true to themselves—
Utterly faceless like brick or wood.
Death is one loud party.
The only substance is the voice
And in each language, you can finally hear.

After the Parade

Outside it is blank and hungry as winter.
Children are waiting, always,
For the clowns and soldiers to return.

That craving,
As if we need to breathe
The breath of the birds,

As if the people we love are too far
Away to know how to save us.
Our fingertips burn on their faces.

The sky moves closer to the earth.
These strange moths wait
For hours outside the windows like friends.

When I let them in they sleep
On the walls, their wings full of secrets.
By morning, they are dead.

Their limp, bloodless wings lie across the floor
Among the dust and human footprints.
I am careful not to step on them.

There must be a scent in the house,
Something dense and without grace,
Pressed between the walls

And the pages of books that kills them.
They must have wanted more
Than they needed, entering this house

Trying to be human, or to even bother
Knowing what it is that humans do.
Though we are just as reckless.

We too wander like thieves
Into windows, far from the places
We are most comfortable.

Underwater Grave

A terrible place to die,
Weeds stroking her like dead tongues.

The ocean with its black-eyed air,
Still as a grave too deep in the earth.

Salt stirs up blood—cleans it,
And death washes up dry,
Clings to sand, and all its wetness
Bakes into a ginger face, ashless,
Just whole and still with flavor.

Poor Mother with her white stomach
Sinking heavy as the ocean shudders
And strips the face of rocks.

Every wave an arm that grabs air
And dips back down to stir the fish.

Her arms drift like a sea angel
Swallowed by the earth.

Eyes, dried-out seeds once full
Of mist and green, now hollow
And white as coconut shells.

Gold and orange fish dance in her mouth,
Looking for words, a voice, her breath.

They drink air from her hands,
Swim through her velvet hair
That still lives and grows and sings.

And her son, head first out,
Red and burning, slips from her
Thin legs like a fire-filled drum.

And moves from her,
Where no one will look,
Know or name.

Transfiguration of the Golden Bird

From that grave of sea in Thessaly
A great fever looms. Sharp rocks rise
Inexplicably into enormous walls
Beyond the Monastery of Transfiguration.

Could these walls be the work of Caenis?
The virgin who walked these shores alone
Before her body was stolen by Neptune,
And left there naked and infertile.

Was his gift expected to console her—
A man's body, a man's voice, and thighs
Immune to sword, to touch, to love?
Had he believed that she would not

Retain a woman's blood and a woman's heart?
That she would not kill with twice the sense
And twice the fury, then, with the weight
Of mountains on her back, turn trees into golden wings,

Rock into fire, fighting until she cracked the earth—
Leaving nothing behind, nothing but a haze of raw light,
And the sound of fire beating into heaven.
Could he have imagined the second gift?

Woman, bird, man, ghost, all at the temperament's will?
How else to explain these monstrous walls,

Scarred the color of human flesh, the gold nests,
The gold caves, and the restless shadows that scorn the shore?

The Golden Bird has not fallen. She is everywhere—
Her wings of steel, of fire, her impenetrable voice.
For years she waited, dancing on the blade
Before the inferno with death in her mouth,

Then she died again in heaven and left god alone.
Between her legs the sea is a ghost that dies
Only to wake again and burn within its flesh.
And the men sail into her without knowing

The nests and wings and fires
Beneath her sapphire gown.
Drifting like kings with her flesh in their mouths,
Their bodies turn to water.

The soil sweetens with the smell of their hair.
Their instincts still tremble in the bone.
And the virgins walk the shore alone,
Shedding from their bodies against the will of the gods.

Heaven

It is rare for the sun to come here.
The shadow trims itself within the hat.
The moon shifts in its ghost of light.

The stone floor of the cathedral falls
Through the earth. Nothing rises.
Not the smell or the fire or the songs.

Such a small part of yourself belongs to you here,
Like a face in black water, separate
From its wrinkles and its cumbersome voice.

Our hands are like torches, they sizzle
And tear and dig at the surface of the earth
Beneath the trees, beneath the air,

But never through the heart, to the other side.
The ones who once knew you carry you
In their pockets among the pennies and broken bones

So far from their own dreams, it is dangerous to love them.
With history dusted and shiny behind the glass,
Things still happen as they happened.

The horses died after the men, and without hands.
The children of the dead lived without dreams—
Actors that can never exist again

Without becoming terrible,
Without the names
That once belonged to someone else.

Children here are never born,
But they die and die.
We shove them underneath the rocks,

In the gutters, into the black, to make it easier
For them to be stolen. They are not beautiful anymore.
Do we think their bones are too heavy for the angels?

What little reason they leave us with.
The angels hide. They taste us.
When we have nothing to say,

It is because we are tasting them,
That sweet and delicious silence, transparent, pure.
Don't ever let me lose you again.

I think of the thieves, the stars,
Those uncertain swells of space that keep us
Reminded how far from ourselves we are,

And how history should connect each star
Like the bones connect the wrist to the fingers,
Strong and certain, forward.

Why do we always blame the dead?
I cannot say no to the clocks,
Though they are made so

Solid and round and permanent.
They do lie. They do keep us wrong.
The dead never rest. There is never peace.

We love the space love doesn't give us.
Each house has its own light, its own time,
Its own clock. And the dogs drag themselves here,

As if this place is no different from any other.
A dog will answer to most any name
If you have the nerve to touch it.

Good morning, angels. Leave us something familiar.
How I want to touch you, whoever you are,
No matter what you've done. No matter how imperfect.

I won't pretend you are invisible. I won't erase you.
I live. I shouldn't complain. I live
And nothing around me crumbles.

A Place We Briefly Lived

The gates are stained with the breath of ghosts.
There's always trouble in the background,
The smell of the dead man's coat; ash
And old church wine. It's disheartening
To think I loved him here, too late into winter
To find charm in the snow. We become bored
Long before we are able to love.

Now that the birds have died,
I am anxious to become myself.
He can tell by now I'm afraid of them.
The shape of their hands, families of ghosts
Quivering like steam and fins of light, seaward.
Our faces are smudged with rumors.
Whatever it is he has lost, I cannot touch.
I am listening to his heart underwater,
In the sea, so quiet it's as if I've hardly lived
Below the earth, where the pulse of the water
Sounds nothing like a heart,
But of a place you will never know well.

Letters from Our Fathers

The foyer is wallpapered with gray
Photos of dead men Father knew.
Statues of gold animals—lions
And dogs guard the voiceless hall,
Their mouths full of rain and blood,
Throats dark and clogged as chimneys.
He keeps no shelves for books,
Newspapers, or sheets of music.

An organ, as if it were a boundary,
Covers a wrinkle in the carpet
That leads to the back door.
And the backyard is still unplanted—
Barrels of unseeded grass, carrots, and banana trees.
He wants to keep a new country there
With roosters, alligators, and eels,
As if guarding the living makes them live longer.

The letters in our pockets remind us
Of the spices in the courtyards, mothers and fathers
With bowls and silverware in their hands,
The sky meditating until it burned down.
And we carried pools of sunlight
In our hands and on our faces
Until our bodies were heavy as prayers.

The Our Father was a sacred song
To some strange man who had died,

Though we were never told many men would
And for lesser reasons—men who cried
Until thunder seemed impossible.

And nobody listened. Our fathers,
Their faces black and blue, stern and old,
Knowing everything except themselves.
We collect their bodies like broken clocks.

Before the blindness our fathers built us playgrounds.
They dug holes and filled them with sand.
When they dreamt of us, we swung back and forth
On the swings until we washed our hair with stars.

Whoever wrote the letters in our pockets—
Poems, testimonies, queries—
Never thought we'd still carry them.

Though they fought gracefully, knowing
Any instrument of memory is useful,
And any official document is a good one.

For hundreds of years, we have remembered
Graveyards are a good place to play.
We were never told it was bad manners
To walk on the dead.
But we know it isn't safe to play after dark.

Our bones are carried, in coffins and cradles,
To the darkest parts of the earth,
While our vows, our lies, the color of our faces
Sprout like weeds in other people's hands.

Away

The sky has an awful way of dressing you,
Cursing and creeping like a suspicious mother.
Now that its bulb has burnt out in the dream
I steal from my mother, taking more
Than she could have given me.
I force my way past the judge, past my father.
I have stolen but my clothes are still made of paper.

America is buzzing in my head, the cruel late-night bass,
The brittle pain of emptied hearts and discontent,
The bad behavior, the spokes, the gravel, the speed—
The perpetual earthquake. How I resemble you,
A similar thief, a blind savage.
So many streets, no one has to teach you how to take.
I ask about the danger here because I can't stop. Snakes?
    Tornadoes?

But with clarity, breathing in this well-tempered air,
I love also what I know can't be loved.
And with the dark sea between us brimming with time,
I defend you—the noise of every country you hold,
The thick, trembling river still balancing, conversing,
Working itself out.

Home

The bulbous white lily came alone,
Appeared after one night,
Like the ghost of a dead sister inviting me home
To the window above the winter garden.
Home now is not a room in my mother's house,
It is the city in itself, any part of it.
The old, silver bridge that masks the green water,
The statues of unknown artists, the lunatics, the toy ships.
Home is knowing my place in Father's new family,
And after we measure and discuss the success of our lives,
Everyone comes up short. Not one of us has it all.
And whoever pretends best gains nothing.

To exist there now, I remember time as it was not lived,
And sculpt away at the faulty faces, recreating a past
Where leftover, unloved things have settled,
And my unrecognizable face and body
That has died many times, that has believed
Other men were her father, can see now
The grace and permanence of birth,
The way a place leads you and in the end doesn't let you go.

The Little Red Schoolhouse

We drew pictures in the window's breath,
Driving where they made us go,
Past apple gardens and fresh fields of air.

Her heavy eyes of sky
Saw freckles near the moon.

Now stars are stars.

New cracks in the wall of my sister
Who slept in the same sheet of skin
As I did for just as long.

She is still young in my eyes
Though her soul is a glacier.

Every nail I punch into the wall
To hang a pretty new painting,

I wish I were nailing her back
To when she didn't know Dad
Would leave and Mom would go crazy.

How can I be happy
Knowing of her dark blood
And scattered head?

I want to wrap her eyes
With bandages,
Push her backwards
To the little red schoolhouse

When we all walk her
To the front door,
And kiss the quiet skin
On her forehead.

Different Ideas of Honor

He hunts through other people's lives,
Counting the days left in his.
Between the doorsteps and the graveyards,
There's always something he can't see.

An old sadness, back again, an old friend dies
Who hadn't been a friend in years,
So he prefers to stay still, cut off,
Worried few people will attend his funeral.

Father, I found the books in the basement,
The blank pages just before the preface
Where women had signed their names
So you'd never forget them. Imagine that!

And you spoke Latin and lived alone
In the desert with books of poetry.
This was before you knew anything difficult,
Of course, when to be so loved meant much less,

When your voice was cool as water, and you hadn't
Yet smothered your life with selfish women.
It is strange that a daughter must always knock
At her father's door. You don't think I remember

When you left us. For years, every Saturday
You hid behind a tree in the dark, looking in

On what would have been your life.
Of course I knew you couldn't have stayed.

What is it you wanted for us, staying in this town
Because there's nowhere else you feel important?
Fifty years of trouble! I worry when I leave,
I may not be back to see you walk

Among the flowers with your palms full of rain,
Passing the church steps you've never walked on.
Telling you isn't enough for you
To believe you are important.

You ask me to play a song for you.
What is music when you don't feel
There's anywhere to go, when there's too much
You won't have to ever be happy?

Hour by hour pieces of light are vanishing.
Soon, your sweet mother will lie in your lap
And sing in your ear again of wizards and crickets.
They will take you and you will laugh again.

Just as you gave a man your old uniform and hurried
In plain clothes back to the town where you were born,
With stars falling through your hands, you will wish
That what you never finished will finish itself.

Stained Dresses

Never thought I'd have to watch her die
Stroking her skin in gold-framed mirrors,
Lifting sacred old sweaters and slips to her face
Hidden in top drawers to fasten the smell.

She still hasn't learned to light the fire herself,
Or brush through the length of her hair.
Nothing can penetrate her senses to smell
The dust on the photo albums or the newspaper scraps.

Her brothers and sisters
Scattered in states she's never been.
In books, she searches for their streets.
What could she do to lure them over now?

Light the window with a Christmas tree,
Order geraniums, grapes, and bright invitations?
Even now, I smell her lonely hands,
Cold as silverware and the shadows

That haunted half the dinner table.
Delirious Mother. Blind Mother.
Talking in her sleep, calling people's names
Over and over as if we're in danger.

Does she pretend to have vanished
As I lift her heavy body from the bath?

38

If a nurse enters, she is still, hoping someone
From her past has come to care about her.

Mother, I never knew the wolves were dead.
The lake rushed around, drunk and heavy
At your feet, and I heard them sing
Like elegant ladies who never sleep.

Empty your pockets and fill them with prayers.
There are no more costumes.
I'll stain your ironed dresses
And invent the places you wore them.

Refugee

I.

When you come back to what you think is home,
The stalls will be cracked and empty of their horses,
The streams scaled with weed and rock.
A dense draught will pour through the church
Strange as a prisoner giving birth.

How many times do you have to die here?
How many old lovers need to touch you again?

At first you came only to smell the winter leaves,
But now you want to take back everything;
The dogs sleeping in the caves,
The fat white birds circling the fields like ghosts.

You'll want to know how to pray.
The dead are long gone, and have left nothing for you.
Not even their bones.

The spiders have vanished from their yellow leaves.
The yellow leaves too have vanished.
The church has no address.

When your fingers touch the doorbell,
That thing that hurts in your heart,
That silence no voice can undo . . .

The houses you built, the stairs,
The people are gray as photographs,
And if you go to them they will fall and break.

II.

If I could take you back to that place I found you—
To the hills where all the dead flowers
Still smell like your hands . . .

If I'd told you I wanted to be honest
When it took us the entire night
To part from the last small town
Where we never used our names . . .

Would it surprise you to know
If you've forgotten my name again,
I don't mind.

III.

You have always been able to fool me,
And to keep you amused, I could pretend
Very well that I didn't know what to expect.

In that space between us at night—
That pool of privacy
Where everything said and unsaid
Has a body and a language of its own—

I have tried to fill it
With plans and memories,
With noise and with my body.

I have been a difficult woman.
I have taken away much of your time.
You only give so much—that part of you
That has only existed in this country.
The rest of you remains across the sea,
And exists only in the landscapes you know—

In the city that isn't tall enough for echoes,
The custard faces of the drunk ladies
Cursing in the kitchen, heaps of bread
And crust on the walls,
The paths that swing into cathedrals,
The prayers and songs still perched on pianos.

Though if I were to sing them to you,
They would mean something different.
The words would wrap around
The hollows of your ears,
But would never get through.

Lament

Well, friend, the room is empty now.
The last logs from the winter fires have burned.
There was little you could have left behind, a name,
The tree you adored that grew twice around itself.
If I wrote to you it would seem too late,
And no one knows, or would have known,
That I steal the ghosts from the river
And look for you in places you'll never go.

So all that is true will stay unheard and less true.
All my obvious words are no longer useful.
But someone can hear me writing them through the night
Like the music that is always the secret of the birds.
The room is empty now, of our cowardly voices,
Of our secrets. I sit under the old lamp until the swallows
Lose their eyes and fold between the stones
Like love we should have made.

Unpolished Houses

I could kill for what you give her,
How you bathe her in the frost
Of pears and orchids, freeing
Angels from your long, warm tongue.

Do you know where I am?
Carrying these indecent words
Back to Venice to pray beside the candles
White and red, for the patriarchal soul,

And those lovely dark trains,
Sure as your hands
Dancing through the piazza,
Covered up like nuns

Before those eternal orchestras.
There's no one I want
To know here, this strange,
Clean air where people sleep.

Climb again, breathe
The barbaric cold of the ice caves.
Where were we going,
The Black Forest?

To sleep on the limbs of frozen trees,
Arguing about God,
Pretending to be children.

Did I know who you were then?

You exquisite man—souls swollen
In your fingertips, eyes gold
And bare as Italian trumpets.

Don't let them close.
I am here.
I remember.

The Burial of Two Strangers

I.

A man is being cremated. The smoke from his stale body
Swells the air like a river of ink. This field is so full
Of ill moods, all that can stop it is sleep.

All the things we've tasted today have left us forever
Smothered with someone else's death. The layers
Of the day repeat themselves street by street, voice by voice,

Reminding us of people missing from our lives.
The sky recedes with broken lights.
All things living up there move past like a pool of dust.

In a chair, a frightened and elegant child plays
With the drama of her black dress, loosening the stitches
To pass time, amused by her own loneliness,
Thinking of ways to read people's minds.

A priest raises a tiny, crystal box and pours the pretty dust
Into the river. This makes the girl happy.

Afterwards, the guests eat watermelon and grapes,
Some get drunk and are afraid to laugh. The girl
Begins to think her new dress makes her look older.

46

A married man thinks another man's wife is beautiful.
He wonders if he'll die jealous of what other men have.
The dead man's cousin is tired.

He's not in the mood for watermelon.
The dead man's mother finds a tear in her stocking.
She hopes no one will notice.

II.

In the same field, a few stones over, a woman has gone mad.
She is throwing things in a casket; letters and photos.
As it lowers, she lays a compass on his chest.

*"Don't look at the clock anymore.
If you need to believe the leaves are white, believe it."*

The young widow has a flower in her hair.
Her face will grow to look like someone she never liked.

The sky knows it is disturbing. So many possible openings.
The moon dangling like a childhood dress,
Spilling the light of memory.
It was there no matter what you did.
No matter where you were.

III.

Skipping through the bedrooms of the dead,
History hangs from the trees,
Cursed and crowded—a chamber-full of blind birds,
Useless as broken fingers.

The world is so full of things that can never belong to us;
A stranger's version of love, his loneliness, his death.

War Tribes

I.

In America we are selling the stars
To our mothers. We have always believed
They were ours, and don't know why

We leave things behind. It is a terrible habit
To believe something you can't even touch
Should belong to you.

Everybody on these streets
Has been left by someone. Lamps hang above
The doorways in case the ones who left return.

The ones who left do return, only to gaze in
The windows, bewildered and impolite, their heads
Full of new love and lamb and yellow pepper.

II.

There are places where sand of black and red glass
Leaks into the north like a fable, fickle and eyeless,
Riding the water like a horse's back, to an island

That gives like heaven—a bouillabaisse of hands and hearts.
A cold smoke covers the battlefields, blurring
The shades of the earth: brown, lily, basil.

White boats carry macadamia and mango.
Men in wicker skirts lay them in the garden,
Delicately as sleeping owls, so the tongues
Of the children stay sweet to sing prayers
In the choir at dark.

III.

Far in the woods,
Past the woodpecker's wild breath,
Before you come upon the words,

Quiet hangs lusciously in your ears
Like the soreness of salt, the pulse
Of a swelling sea, then their voices

Prowl upon you like bleeding angels,
So harmless and drunk,
They make you think you're God.

Every man is both your child and father.

IV.

The tribe sheds its skin
To see if its blood is black.
Some will claim their blood is white

To sleep in a straw house past the hills,
And use their old, old hands only to feed
The corpse, a dead child with green eyes,

As jade is considered a holy stone,
A color that gleams of fertility.

V.

They don't know there are places
Where the stars have already been sold.

VI.

America. Not even the stars are free.
Clocks break in our hands.
Angels bleed in our heavy, silver hair.
Like a maze of wires, we hurry
To the crust of fruitless cities, watching
To see who's watching us. Measuring
Our lives against the dazzling dresses of monarchs.

We are the reigns of monsoons,
We are the floggers and drivers.
Like ironfisted statues,
We have drowned the world.

With Dutch gold cradles we move
From shoe to shoe, boots to slippers,
Hauling picture frames in our pockets,
Saving portraits of our lives,
Insisting they be buried with us.

Old Soldiers

The room is dark,
Except for your hearts.

Anything you can't have
Sets an obvious darkness onto your faces.

You dead fools,
Trodding about slow as ducks

With spoons stuck in your necks
Pretending to be human.

You have died again and again.
You have had birthdays with strangers.

This time you will die pretending not to care.
This time you will die well.

There will be cliffs and bells and apricots.
There will be one small sea to drink all at once.

Ghosts, you lonely, radiant creatures,
It is your night. I will praise only you.

I will carry your hats and suits and dreams
And hang them over every church

Like a pile of moonlight mistaken for a child.
I will carry you, old soldiers—

Your cards and games, your children.
I will carry you as perfectly as a thief.

Still I will know nothing about you.
I would not even want to bring you home

Where the warm schoolhouse walls hang
Nothing but maps.

Sleepwalking

And the last star will vanish
Before daylight crosses his mind.
To sleep while awake,
Thawing in a casket
Still as a book or a frozen lake.
To spend time on time,
Thirsty as a poet on the verge of death—
A liar with nothing to lie about,
As the lights fall, one by one, off the earth.

The Neighbor's Will

The man downstairs is weeping
In a room of leftover cravings,
Spoiled bread and liquor,
Holding on to strangers,
Imagining himself dead,
Eyes beaten in,
Bruised like rotten apples.

Though the centers are brisk
As the morning horns and bells
That never fail to wake him.
There are places he could go,
But he is ill, brotherless,
And the little women down the road
Who bring him tea are too old
To walk that far.

If he knew any better
He wouldn't be here,
Throwing open windows,
Praying for cracks in the sky.
For miles, vultures fall
Like scraps of burnt paper,
Smooth as liquor
In their lavender wings,
Biting through strips of air—
A waterfall of hands

Delicate as the women
Who used to move his furniture
Around and plant him vegetables
In their ageless, white dresses
That hung on the clothesline
For years, impotent as wet paper.

Painting the Dead

Old woman,
Hands rough as walnuts,
Gathers flowers and straw,
Sews fresh wreaths to every wall.

No strength in the scent of death.
Corpses in and out of the house,
Delivered at all hours, driven
Alongside fresh bread trucks.

Something is still alive
Within the smell, a voice.

Painting the dead:
One will ask her
To tighten a bandage
Or get them a snack.

She soothes their heads,
Makes them up prettier
Than they've ever looked.
First time on stage, young child?

She sleeps with the smell
Of dead love on her hands.
Washing only rubs it in.

Old men who die lonely rest with larger stomachs.
Young men who die alone are thin.
A man's hand has larger scabs
Only because the hand is larger.

Women have more bruises
Only because the skin bruises better.
Worried women have thinner jawbones.
Old women have cleaner feet.
Young women never die well.

If the fist is closed, they are happy to leave.
If the fist is open, there was much left to do.

Washing only moves it around.

Exit

When night picks itself up
Dropping dying birds upon us,

And people order us to go somewhere,
Tight-lipped with our hands full of papers;

Remember, we grow at the pace of our own hearts,
And it's laughter that spins us forward,

So spread me over the world first.
Take my fingers and fold them around

Heads that need direction.
Press my lips to the hands of anyone

Who has never been loved.
Turn my voice into strains of heat.

If there's quiet near you too often,
You might have your back turned on someone.

You may be loving only half
Of something and never know it.

Forget I was wrong when I was.
If I lied let it teach you something.

Carry my eyes into the dusk.
Match me up with a hand-shaped clock.

If you hear a strange sound in the closet,
Let the darkness of it be me.

Like Silk

Gone so long
Forgot where the light switches are.
Grandfather is definitely dead.
Died years ago.
No curtains on the kitchen window.
No new Grandfather living there.
The yard once full
Of tomatoes and spices
Dead and leafless.
No one to dig up the roots,
Keep them wet.
Sits like winter.
Pots overturned
On the back steps
Once filled with tea and lime
Shelter cold birds.
Streetlights go on
Only if you walk past.
It's always too cold
To walk past.

Blackstone Street

There are people I don't want to see my blood in.

Doors open and behind them nothing is open
But sprouts of trees, wood for coffins to load up the man.

I am only cold winds bathing; remnants—
Ashes of troubles and clothes.

If the blood is clean I won't touch it.

The end is never clean,
Even how the children remember you.

Perhaps I should wear you once, Father,
And walk the streets where they killed you.

The Church of St. Sulspicious

This town is always scattered with snow
Gray as the dust of bones.

At the trainstop. Near the fires.
If you breathe too deeply

You'll inhale the ash.
From the walls of the church,

The prayers of gin-soaked men—
Two-headed soldiers pouring their souls

Over the square abbey farms, watering
The garden with their own blood.

The scraps of the dead still burn in their mouths.
Graveyards with names and names.

From the high seas, the estranged glow of angelfish
Like spiritual nurses with lanterns and tools,

As if to say life will come for you again,
Light up and hand you new windows.

We pass ourselves out—hold ourselves hostage,
Always looking to the birds that land freely,

Dropping a feather like a sad word,
Shielding the light with their threadlike wings

Waving, tugging at us like tambour and bagpipes.
A band of soldiers sewing us into the sky's church.

Into the lens. The contour lines. Filling our mouths
With ghosts, stranding us in our cribs.

The Man at Her Window

If you walk past her house
When it is just becoming night

And the bloodless night-birds pour
Onto cathedrals quietly as stone,

All the white tablecloths will be
Painted with fruit and cream and dust,

The orchard will be damp and radiant,
The puppets and dolls brushed and buckled.

For a moment,
You will see her dancing with him

And you might not notice
The lilies asleep on the windowsill,

Their buds bent forward like a frozen waterfall.
Dreams breaking off into the cold.

Burdened by the clock, the sound of her chair
That ticks like a clock, the stray dogs at her door,

The boys asleep on the hill, their bare heads,
Their dumb, eager hands.

Though she will never know you,
Without her you will never love anyone.

You will always be a fool with pale, limp hands,
So you may as well touch her.

You may as well let her know you are there.

The Squirrel

Each time I come across you
When the earth is most fresh and bare,
And the living seem to never end,

You dash across the windowsills
Of my life with your fat, gold fingers
And your legs full of fire.

I can tell you have lived a long time
By the terrible way you look at me, cursed
As a dog that smells and hears everything.

I follow you carefully with handfuls of nuts,
Spilling them like rain over your footprints.
You turn to look, but refuse to take

What I want to give you.
Maybe I'm not what you wanted.
Maybe I shouldn't be living here.

In the weeks that pass,
I gather pieces of your life
Like dead, green leaves.

As the hair sheds from your brittle head
Prematurely as these ghostly leaves,
You must think of what shows on my face—

The incongruities, the fear
Of my decisions finally crumbling.
You think of me,

And the invisible webs
In every corner of this house.
Though I know you want to

Carry me like a basket of nuts,
Up to your iridescent trees,
You do not have the strength or the arms.

Afterlife

This boy, what he seems
To be now, my husband.
Within his silence are the many lives
Of a listless boy I wish I'd seen
From a porch across the street
When he didn't know I was looking.

And his shoes would be untied,
Heavy with dreams and sadness
And I'd know why
His father's hands were so cold.
But he sleeps where he is sleeping
Behind the color of my eyes.

And I don't know how
To keep him laughing.
Comfort is too old for me,
But it creeps in
Like an old lady's shoes
With no color or flavor.

And there is nothing
In his fingertips
But the hot dark salt
Between other women's legs
As he cooks up
The heat in their breath.

The Habit

I.

Our yard is a mystery. Wallflowers leaking
From the brick like umbilical cords.
Everyone who walks there must see something
About us that we don't. Labeling thoughts
Like drawers. Gluing them shut.
Tremendous hallways. Walls of pigmented gray
Fingerprinted by women's fretted hands.

The heart of this house is beyond its time.
We may as well leave the curtains open.
Now I'm sure you have to tell me why
The windows are smaller than my eyes
And the draught so heavy it freezes ideas.

II.

None of this, not the luscious watercolors,
Or the dainty, pastel rugs,
Not the curtains that push daylight
Into tiny threads of white and blue,

Or the many sheets of paper
On the table in this room is enough.

The hibiscus planted next to the door
Greet a person at the strangest times.
Even in full bloom they are shriveled
And weak as orange peels pulled from the fruit.

I bring so many flowers into this house,
Any new smell to keep the air alive.
But the colors don't exist, and your eyes don't exist
Even when I know they do.

Laugh until the water spills from your mouth,
And there's little of you to recognize.
Be the trumpet without a scar or a scratch. Be anyone.

Sweep me into the broken room
Where the womb never heals,
And your companion is merely an eye.

As you sleep the past is growing,
Toward you, summoning you—
A face on a penny. A shadow from a train.
It's only what doesn't change that amuses you.

III.

The flames wait like a predator's hands
For you to lie again, to me, to yourself,
To take your face through the glass.
I wish I could be the same without forgetting anything
My good heart knows you. I try. My love can't stop you.

Believing in you can't stop you. The door slams.
All of the doors are broken. The walls patched
And covered by books—the stories of other people's lives—
Characters upon characters that never knew themselves,
That only live as someone else needs them to.

IV.

Here you go again, pushing me into the walls
So I use their hearts. Their hearts are like yours
When that funk is in you and all the love you
Put across me in a day becomes a wall.
When I put my clothes in a box,
And search through dyed papers for lines,
You fall asleep first, aware that I'm helpless again.
In your sleep, I'm sure you know it too,
The zoo inside me, the enemy you let out.
I draw more lines, between us, the world,
The cradling walls of this room.

Each time you do this—trade my whole happiness
For five minutes of laughter—you can't be looking ahead,
Entering a stage when you do nothing but bow.
When the hands stop clapping, that's when it's my turn
To watch that layer of skin plunge off you, elevate
And slither up your neck. You become certain
That I am the mother of all men,
And I, like some fallen window,
Pushed you away from yourself, hid you from other women,
Composed your life like an off-key melody,
Put you to bed early, and certainly, left the closet open

So other beasts would find you, and they did, didn't they?
Except you fought them and they became you.

V.

We go to this room, its comfortable old light,
Only when the day has lost its sense,
And with half our breaths,
Exchange what little more we know.
Tomorrow another mistake will lose its wings,
Fall through the air, forget why,
And stain the garden with its own tiny bones.

Months later, while we are sleeping,
Delicate flowers will rise and spread,
Breathing from their own small lights,
Their faces bent to the earth.
We'll assume they are weeds at first,
And as you reach for their necks,
I will call you back into the house,
And I will tell you: If they grow here they belong to us.
We must let them exist as they please.

They may never die,
And will look no different as they grow older,
While age will begin to change our lives.
And as I try to get into your secrets
I will lose more of myself—my friends,
My accent, the characters in these stories.
I will then become some part
Of the character you wished for.

VI.

For years we've lived
Uncertain of our roles,
Uncertain as the shadow maker
And the final shade of the scar.

I am not your wife.
Anyone who knows us knows
Even without these words.
You have brought me here.
Each of my fingers had a name,
An earth, a color of blood, contempt.
Now my hand is one calm web,
Unlit and invisible in an attic or a chimney.

You have brought me here,
But I can still raise my arms.
And in secret or not,
I have never vowed anything to you.
I have never drunk the holy wine,
Or pressed my hands in the holy water.
I still have the birthmark below my knee
That binds me to nothing but my own civility.